Hindu MANDIR

Anita Ganeri

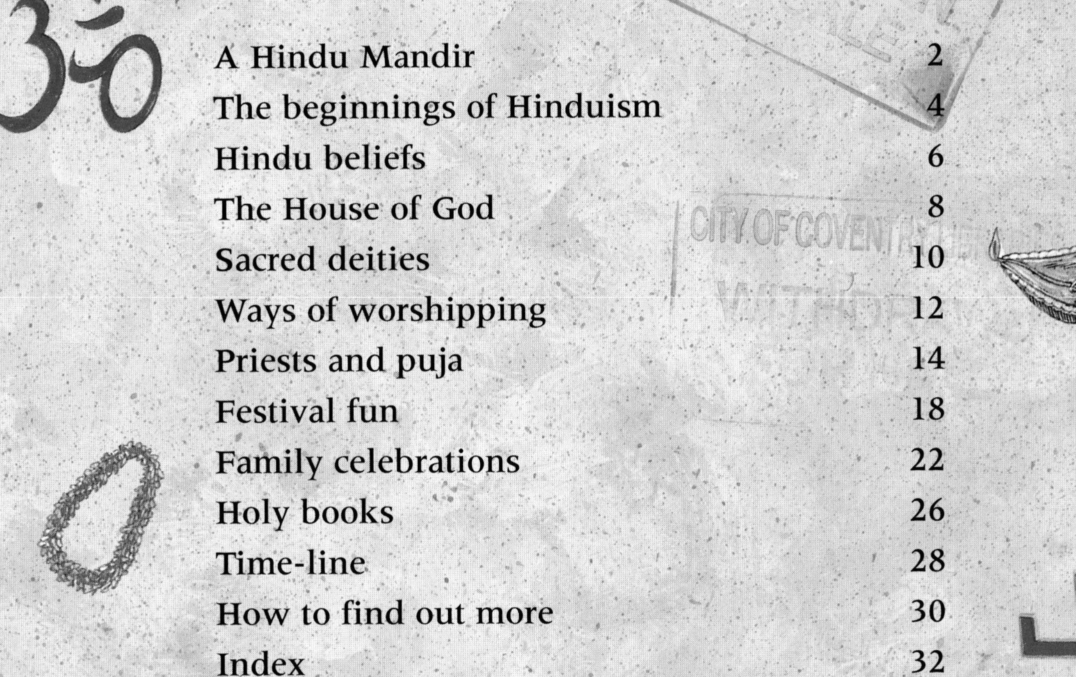

Contents

A & C BLACK • LONDON

A Hindu Mandir

This book is about a Hindu *mandir*, a holy place where Hindus go to worship. The children in this book visited the magnificent Shri Swaminarayan Mandir in Neasden, north-west London. They wanted to find out more about Hinduism, the religion which Hindus follow.

*Each part of the **mandir** has a special meaning. The tiny golden pots on top of the roof pinnacles are said to contain **amrita**, a special potion which gives everlasting life. The seven spires or **shikharas**, represent mountains, carrying people's hopes and prayers upwards to heaven.*

*You can read more about how the **mandir** was built in the time-line on page 28.*

*The children walked up the huge marble staircase to reach the main gateway to the **mandir**.*

The *mandir* was officially opened in August 1995, the first traditional *mandir* to be built outside India. It was constructed according to ancient rules laid down thousands of years ago. This is not the only Hindu *mandir* in Britain – there are many others all over the country, wherever Hindus have settled. But most of these have been set up in community halls, converted churches or even in people's houses.

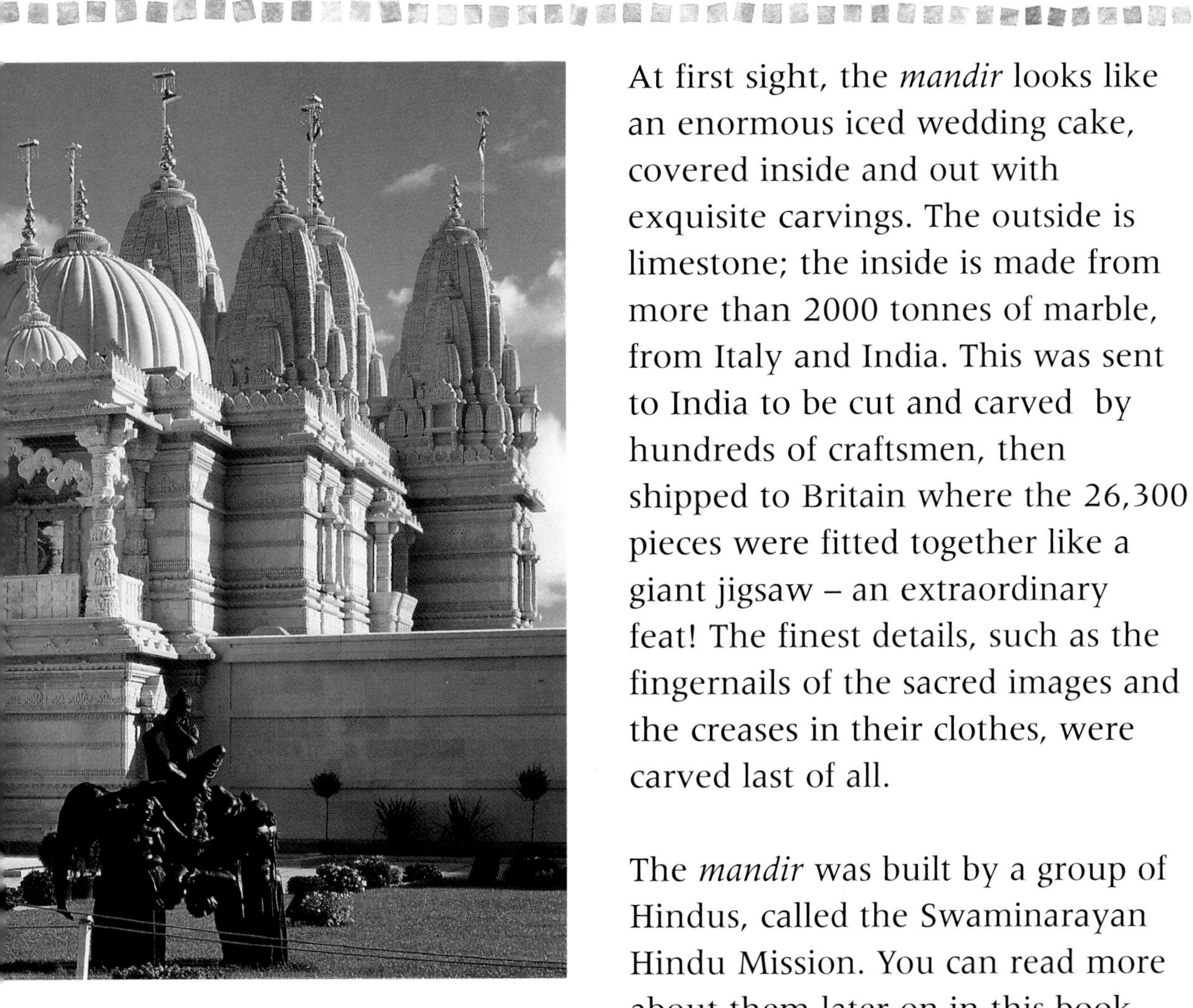

At first sight, the *mandir* looks like an enormous iced wedding cake, covered inside and out with exquisite carvings. The outside is limestone; the inside is made from more than 2000 tonnes of marble, from Italy and India. This was sent to India to be cut and carved by hundreds of craftsmen, then shipped to Britain where the 26,300 pieces were fitted together like a giant jigsaw – an extraordinary feat! The finest details, such as the fingernails of the sacred images and the creases in their clothes, were carved last of all.

The *mandir* was built by a group of Hindus, called the Swaminarayan Hindu Mission. You can read more about them later on in this book. The whole community was involved in the building project, cleaning, providing food for the workers and raising funds. Children raised money by collecting five and a half million aluminium cans from all over the UK for recycling. And everyone can feel very proud of what they have achieved – the biggest and most beautiful *mandir* in Britain, and a wonderful place to investigate.

)n either ide of the teps, there ıre carvings ·f musicians ·laying a song ·f welcome to vorshippers.

The beginnings of Hinduism

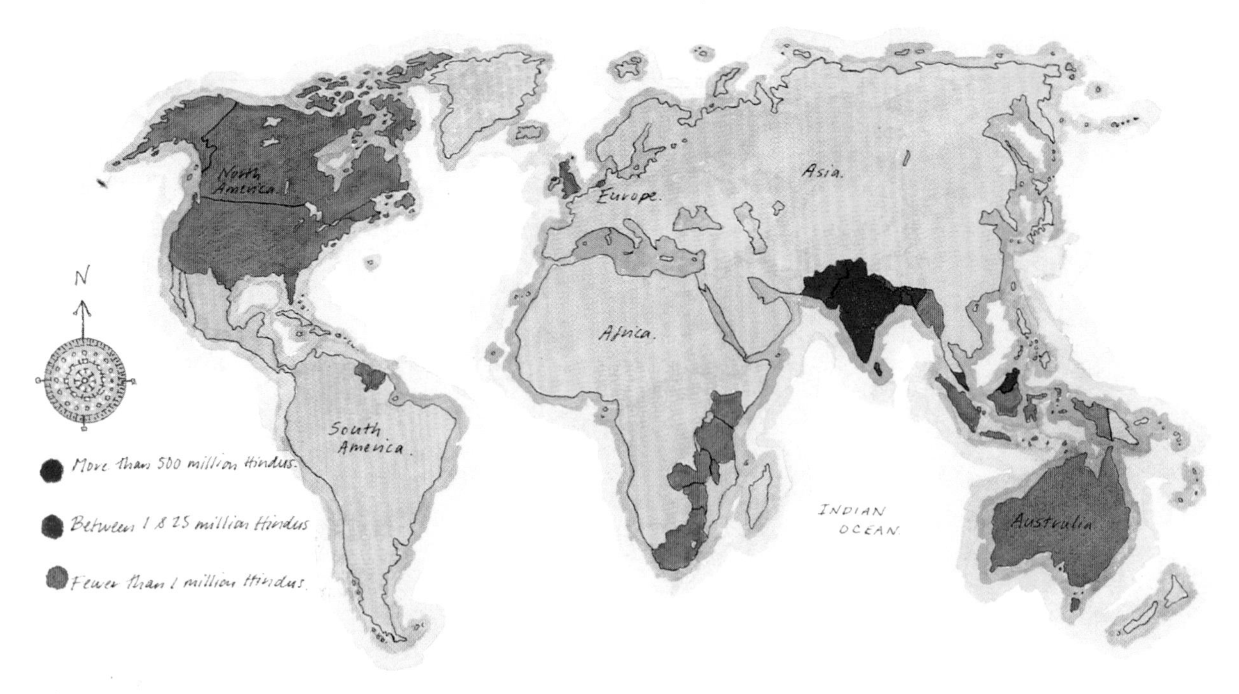

▲ *This map shows where Hindus live. About two thirds of Hindus live where their religion began, in India and the countries around it. But Hindus have also gone to live and work in other countries.*

Hundreds of stone seals have been found in the Indus Valley. Some show sacred animals, such as bulls, tigers and elephants.

Hinduism is one of the world's oldest religions. No one knows exactly when it began but its roots reach back some 5,000 years to the time of the Indus Valley Civilisation.

This mighty civilisation and its people flourished in a region which is now partly in Pakistan and partly in India. Archaeologists have found many clay figures among the ruined cities of the Indus Valley. They believe these show deities similar to those which Hindus worship today.

▲ *There are thousands of* ***mandirs*** *in India. Some are no bigger than garden sheds. Others are much larger and grander. This is the Shri Meenakshi temple in Madurai, south India. Its tall towers are covered in multi-coloured carvings of the deities.*

Today, most Hindus still live in India where their religion began. There are now large Hindu communities in Britain, Africa, North America, the Caribbean and South East Asia. There are about 700 million Hindus in the world. Wherever Hindus have settled they have built mandirs to worship in.

Hinduism is an unusual religion because it was not founded by one person and does not have one single sacred book. Christians, for example, follow the teachings of Jesus Christ and read the Bible. Hinduism is made up of many different strands of belief and worship. You will find out about some of them as you read this book.

nside the ***mandir****, the hildren looked around n exhibition which old them the story of Hinduism from its eginnings in the ndus Valley to the resent day.*

Hindu beliefs

Hindus call their religion *sanatana dharma*, the eternal teaching. It plays an extremely important part in their lives. Rather than being separate from their daily lives, it is seen as a whole way of living, guiding how people live, what they eat and how they see the world.

Hinduism is also a very flexible religion, allowing people to worship in many different ways. Some Hindus try to visit the *mandir* every day. Others only go to take part in special festivals and celebrations. It is left to each person to decide what is best for him or her.

*The children asked what the swastika symbols on the doors of the **mandir** meant. They discovere that the swastika is an ancient Hindu sign of peace and good luck.*

Om is a sacred sound, recited at the start of prayers, meditation and readings from the sacred texts. It is believed to be the first sound of creation and to contain all the secrets of the universe.

This is the dome-shaped ceiling above the inner sanctum, the holiest part of the ***mandir****. The dome represents the sky, from which a person receives divine inspiration.*

Most Hindus, though, share the same basic beliefs. They believe that, when you die, your soul is reborn into another body and lives on. This body may be human or animal. You can be eborn many times. But the quality of your next life depends on how you act in this life.

f you behave well, you will be reborn into a higher form. If you behave badly, you will be reborn into a lower form. This is called *karma*. The aim of a Hindu's life is to break free from the circle of death and rebirth and to reach *moksha*, or salvation.

In Hinduism, making sacrifices for others is highly valued. In the exhibition, the children learned the story of King Rantidev. He was rich and powerful but he was also very generous. Eventually, he gave away his whole kingdom and all his money.

The House of God

Each Hindu *mandir* is dedicated to a deity or an *incarnation* of God who represents God's presence on Earth. The *mandir* is seen as God's home on Earth and a *murti,* or sacred image, of the deity stands in the main shrine of the inner sanctum. Sacred images of other deities stand in smaller shrines on either side.

Hindus visit the *mandir* not only to pray but to have *darshana* of the deity. This means a sight or a viewing of the sacred image in the main shrine. They also make offerings to God, in return for his blessing.

The inner sanctum is the holiest part of the ***mandir****, a peaceful place, decorated from top to bottom with carvings of sacred deities. The children thought it was very beautiful.*

In the main shrine stand the sacred images of Purna Purushottam Lord Swaminarayan (centre), the first Guru, Akshar Brahman Swami Gunatitanand (left), and an important saint, Swami Gopalanand (right).

*On 18 August 1995, the sacred images were carried through the streets of London as part of a colourful procession. They were installed in the **mandir** during a special ceremony two days later.*

The Neasden *mandir* is dedicated to Lord Swaminarayan, who lived from 1781-1830 CE. He is believed to have been an incarnation of God who appeared on Earth in human form to teach his message of peace, love and purity. From an early age, he showed great spiritual powers, mastering the scriptures, performing miracles and eventually founding the Swaminarayan Movement. He also built six beautiful mandirs and set out a code for his followers to live by. His work was continued, after his death, by a series of spiritual leaders, called *gurus*.

The present Guru, Pujya Pramukh Swami Maharaj, is the fifth in line. The movement is based in Gujarat, in western India, but has many followers all over the world. In Britain, it is known as the Swaminarayan Hindu Mission.

*Worshippers gather in front of the main shrine for **darshana** of the sacred images.*

Sacred deities

Hindus believe in God, who they call *Para Brahman*, the supreme spirit. But there are many sacred images in the *mandir*. These deities all represent different aspects of *Para Brahman* and various incarnations in which *Para Brahman* has appeared on Earth.

The deities are often shown with several hands and arms, holding sacred objects which symbolise their special powers.

The most important Hindu deities are Brahma, creator of the universe, Vishnu, the protector, and Shiva, the destroyer. Each has a *consort* and rides on a special animal.

Brahma's *consort* is Saraswati, the goddess of art and literature. Brahma rides on a goose. Vishnu is married to Lakshmi, goddess of luck, wealth and beauty. Vishnu rides on a gigantic eagle. Shiva's *consort* is the goddess, Parvati. Shiva rides on a huge bull, called Nandi.

Shiva is the deity who destroys evil in the world. His right hand is raised in blessing. On his forehead is the third eye of knowledge. The sacred River Ganges flows from his hair. Shiva's ***consort*** *Parvati stands on his left.*

Ganesh, the elephant-headed deity, is Shiva and Parvati's son. He is the patron god of travellers and the god who removes obstacles.The childre found out that Hindus pray to Ganesh whenever they start a new task, such as beginning a new job, attending a new school or building a new ***mandir****!*

Two of the best-loved *incarnations* of God are Lord Rama and Lord Krishna. The children looked at their images in the *mandir*. Lord Rama and Lord Krishna are really the god, Vishnu, in disguise. He appeared on Earth nine times, in nine different forms, to save the world.

Lord Rama is worshipped as a great hero. You can read more about him on pages 19 and 27. Lord Krishna is fond of playing tricks and performing miracles.

▲ *In the inner sanctum, the hildren were shown the image of Ianuman, the monkey-like deity. Ianuman is Rama's loyal friend nd servant. He helps Rama to escue his* ***consort****, Sita, from the vil demon, Ravana.*

'arvati is sometimes gentle and ometimes fierce. This is Parvati in her var-like form as the goddess, Durga, 'iding on her tiger. How many veapons can you see in her hands? ▶

Ways of worshipping

When Hindus visit the *mandir*, the first thing they must do is take off their shoes. This is a sign of respect and purity. Then they walk quietly into the inner sanctum, for *darshana* of the sacred images, and to give offerings of fruits, flowers and to join in with the prayers.

When the children began their visit, they took their shoes off before they went into the inner sanctum. People do this as a sign of respect.

In some mandirs, the main shrine is always open for *darshana*. In the Neasden *mandir*, there are set times of the day when the sacred images can be seen. But you can still visit the inner sanctum in the meantime and enjoy its peaceful surroundings.

*In many **mandirs**, worshippers ring a large bell as they enter and leave to awaken their senses for worship.*

As part of their worship, people walk slowly around the main shrine, along a marble pathway. They always walk in a clockwise direction, keeping their right hands towards the shrine and the images of the gods. This is because Hindus traditionally use their right hands for eating and other "clean" tasks. They use their left hands for washing and "unclean" jobs.

*Hundreds of volunteers were involved in building the **mandir** and now help to look after it. They are happy to give up their time and see it as a way of showing their devotion to God. Some volunteers give guided tours for visitors.*

*The children listened to the story of how the **mandir** was built. Other volunteers help with the cleaning, cooking, run the bookshop or mind the cloakroom and shoe racks.*

When Hindus worship, make offerings or say their prayers, this is called *puja*. *Puja* can be performed by priests in the *mandir*, or by people in their own homes. Many Hindus perform *puja* at home, in the morning and again in the evening. The whole family joins in.

Many Hindus set aside a room or quiet area at home as a shrine. Here they make offerings to a sacred image or a picture of a deity.

Priests and puja

Each Hindu *mandir* has its own group of priests who perform the *puja* ceremonies and look after the sacred images. Some also conduct special ceremonies, such as weddings and funerals. Some priests visit people's homes to cast horoscopes and recite prayers and passages from the scriptures. The priests who perform *puja* are called *pujaris*. Religious teachers and holy men are often given the honorary title of *Swami*.

These sadhus, or holy men, are singing ***bhajans****, hymns of praise to God. At present, there are 11 sadhus in the* ***mandir****.*

This is the spiritual leader, or Guru, of the Swaminarayan Movement, Pujya Pramukh Swami Maharaj performing the morning ***puja*** *at the* ***mandir****. He is wearing saffron-coloured robes, the holy colour of Hinduism.*

Some priests lead very strict lives, dedicated to prayer and devotion. They are called *sadhus*, or holy men. The *sadhus* of the Swaminarayan Movement have to take five strict vows. They are not allowed to get married or to have any money or possessions. They must give up any attachments to their families or homes. They must have no personal tastes or preferences. Finally, they must stay free from pride and anger.

When worshippers arrive for *darshana*, they bring flowers, fruit, sweets and incense to offer to the sacred images. These offerings are called *prasad*.
The *pujari* takes them and offers them to the images to be blessed by God. Then the *pujari* gives them back to the worshippers to bestow God's blessings on them.

*For festivals and other religious ceremonies, Hindus use a special calendar of 12 months, based on the phases of the Moon. This fantastic display of **prasad** has been specially prepared for the Hindu New Year's Day celebrations in the **mandir**.*

*The display of **prasad** is called **annakut**. Hundreds of types of food are given as offerings to God to thank him for providing food throughout the year.*

At the end of the *puja*, the priest performs another ceremony, called *aarti*. A special tray is prepared, with a lamp with five wicks. This is waved clockwise in a circle in front of the shrine while the worshippers sing a hymn of praise. Then the worshippers hold their hands over the sacred fire and touch their faces with its warmth. In the Neasden mandir, *aarti* is performed five times a day, starting just before dawn and finishing in the evening.

*Here Pujya Pramukh Swami Maharaj performs **aarti** at the temple's opening. You can see the tray of lamps in the foreground.*

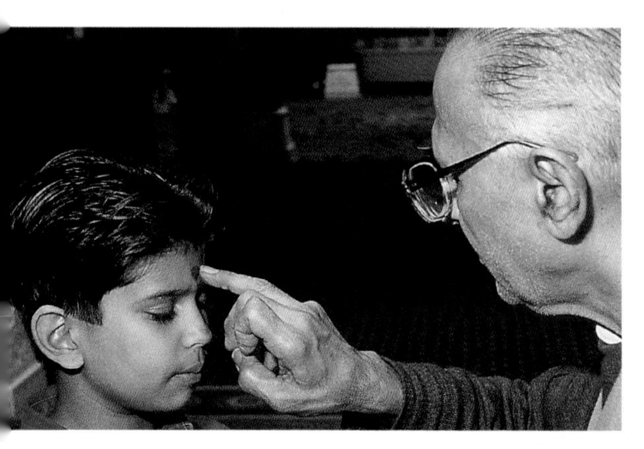

*After the **puja**, the priest marked Dylan's forehead with a red mark of blessing, called a **chandlo**.*

The sacred images in the *mandir* are treated like living beings. As honoured guests, they must be well looked after. Early each morning, they are woken up and dressed in fine clothes and jewellery. Then they are offered breakfast. At about 11 a.m., they are given a tray of food for lunch. They rest in the afternoon, then they are woken again and offered fresh fruit to eat and juices to drink. Later in the evening, after dinner, they are dressed in their nightclothes, ready to go to bed. On special occasions, the images are bathed in a mixture of milk, sugar, *ghee* and honey.

*Outside many **mandirs** in India, there are stalls where you can buy colourful garlands like these.* ▼

The children made a beautiful garland of fresh flowers. Garlands may be offered to God or given to guests as a sign of welcome. ▶

Festival fun

The children bought some special sweets from the ***mandir*** *shop. People often give sweets as gifts at festival times. The sweets are usually made of milk, sugar, nuts and coconut.*

There are hundreds of Hindu festivals, large and small, throughout the year. These are celebrated both in India and by Hindus living abroad. Some mark special events in the lives of the deities. Others are linked to important times of the year, such as the coming of spring, or the harvest. The whole family visits the *mandir* at festival times. A special *puja* is held, sweets and gifts are exchanged and there is often music and dancing. At the *mandir*, the children heard the stories of the two main Hindu festivals — Holi and Diwali.

The highlight of the Holi festival is drenching your friends, parents and even your teachers with coloured powders and water. Even the sacred images are sprayed with colour.

Holi

The festival of Holi marks the end of winter and the arrival of spring, when farmers celebrate the first harvest of the year. On the night before Holi, bonfires are lit to burn models of the evil witch, Holika. Legend says that she was burned to death when she fell into a fire which she had intended to be for her nephew. In Krishna's time, Holi was celebrated by throwing coloured powders and water over people. This custom continues today, on the day of Holi itself. In the evening, people change into their best clothes and visit their relatives with gifts of sweets.

)iwali

)iwali is the Hindu festival of lights, celebrated in late October or early Jovember. In India, it lasts for five days. In Britain, festivities usually last or one evening only, on the Saturday nearest Diwali, with fireworks and special feast. During Diwali, people light lamps at home and in the *nandir*, to celebrate Rama's home-coming after his long years in exile. ₹ama's story is told in a long poem called the *Ramayana*.

The son of King Dasharatha, Rama and his wife, Sita, are banished to the forest by his wicked stepmother. One day, while Rama is out hunting, Sita is kidnapped by the demon king of Lanka, the ten-headed Ravana. Rama is heartbroken. With the help of his trusty friend, the monkey general, Hanuman, he sets out to rescue her. Many adventures later, Rama leads his army across the sea to Lanka. A terrible battle follows in which Rama fits a golden arrow to his bow and shoots Ravana straight in the heart. Then he and Sita return home, their exile over, to be crowned king and queen. Their home-coming brings a time of love, peace, harmony and righteousness.

The children learned that Diwali is also a time vhen business people offer ***puja*** *to Lakshmi, oddess of wealth and good fortune. This picture hows an accounting ceremony when people start heir new account books for the year to come.*

Many festivals are celebrated with special meals for family and friends. Some *mandirs* provide food for worshippers and have a small shop selling sweets, snacks and vegetables. In the Neasden *mandir*, worshippers enjoy a sumptuous meal after celebrating festivals or special occasions. A meal is also provided every Saturday.

Every Saturday in the kitchen at the ***mandir****, volunteers prepare vast quantities of rice, dal and vegetable curry.*

Volunteers serve a meal during the Ram Navmi festival. To accommodate the huge number of visiting devotees, women and children eat in the gym at the ***mandir****, and the men eat outside in a marquee.*

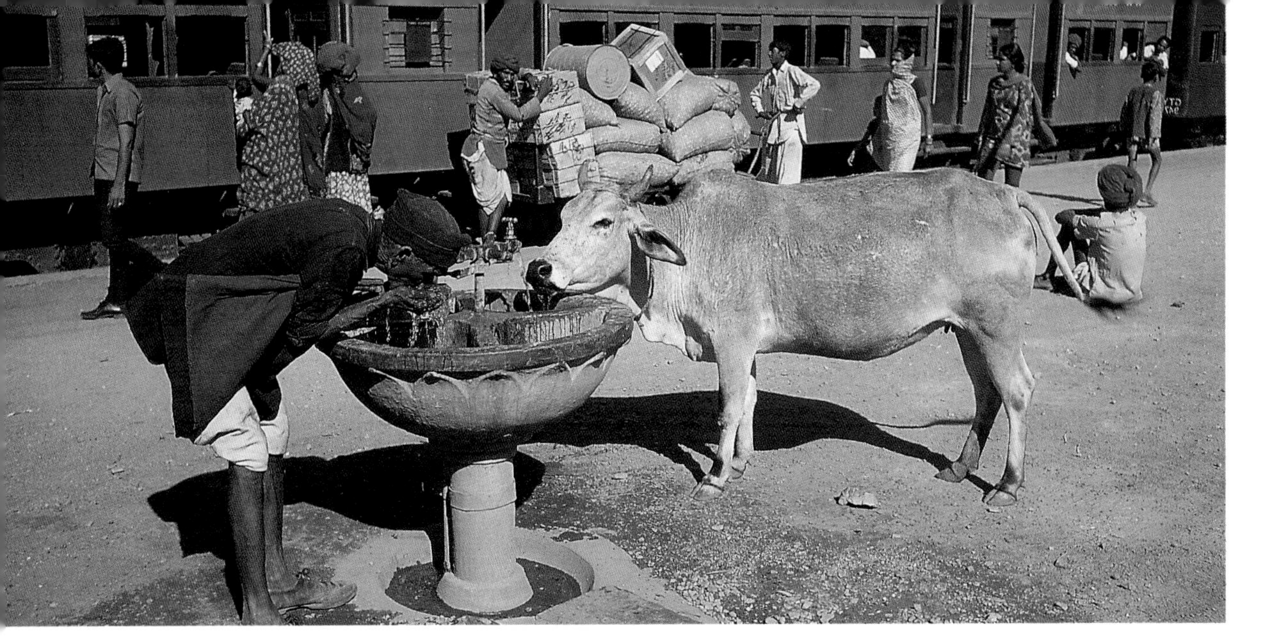

ı India, sacred cows wander the streets. Nobody will hurt or kill them.

Aost Hindus are vegetarians. They have respect for all living things nd do not believe in killing them to eat. Some people do eat chicken, r fish, particularly if they come from regions near the sea. But Hindus ever eat beef. They believe that cows are sacred animals because they rovide milk, a precious source of nourishment.

)ther festivals involve fasting, r going without food. :hildren and people who are ld or sick are allowed to eat ome food, such as milk and ruit. At the Neasden *mandir,* levotees fast every 15 days. 'hey may eat just once during he day, eat only fruit or drink nly water. On five special lays in the year, they do not at or drink at all. Fasting ielps to focus all their energy nto worshipping God.

James looked at the fruit and vegetables on sale in the ***mandir*** *shop.*

Family celebrations

For Hindus, family life is very important. In India, many Hindus live as part of a large family, with several generations sharing the same house and helping to look after each other. In Britain, families are often smaller but family ties are just as close. The many special celebrations in a Hindu's life are a chance for the whole family to get together.

Here the Guru is performing ***aarti*** *with a group of children in the prayer hall.*

Hundreds of worshippers have gathered in the prayer hall. Communal prayers take place five times a day. They start with prayers and the singing of ***bhajans****. This is followed by readings from the scriptures.*

Many family celebrations take place in the *mandir*. The *mandir* is not simply a place for worship. It is much more than that. At Neasden, there is a huge prayer hall with room for 2,500 worshippers, a sports hall, a marriage hall, conference centre and library, apart from the *mandir* itself. People come to celebrate, meet their friends and relations, study the scriptures and learn more about their religion.

he first celebration in a
indu's life takes place even
efore a baby is born,with
rayers for its health and
appiness. More ceremonies
llow over the next few
ears to mark its birth,
aming, first outing and first
aircut, all presided over by
priest.

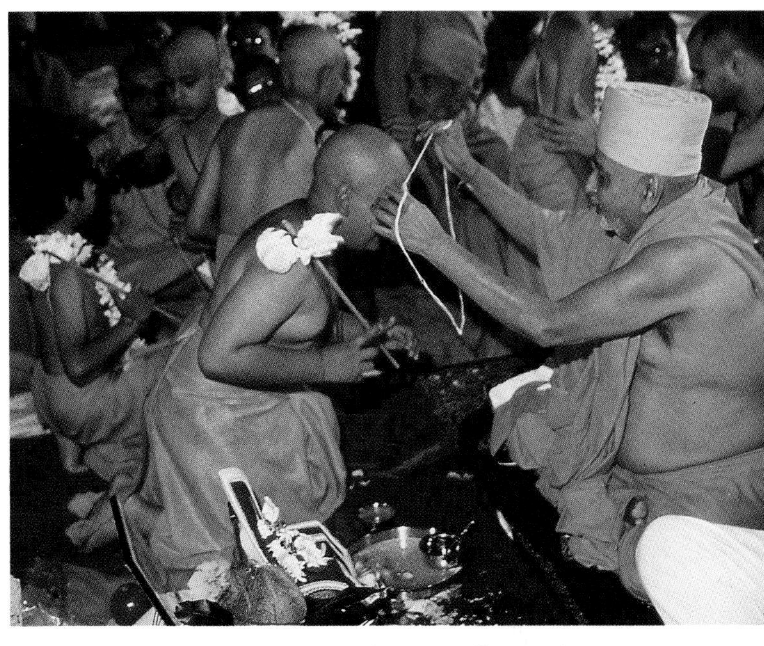

*A sacred thread ceremony in the **mandir**. In the past a Hindu boy would have left his family home and gone to live with his guru to be educated. This does not happen today, but boys still carry white bundles on sticks throughout the sacred thread ceremony. The bundles contain food for the journey to the guru which they would once have made.*

he priest also casts a
oroscope, which shows
ne position of the stars
nd planets on the baby's
irthday. Horoscopes are
onsulted to fix lucky dates
r weddings and so on later
n life.

*he sacred thread is changed once a year after a short eligious ceremony at the **mandir**.*

When a Hindu boy is about 10 years old, he receives his sacred thread from the priest. This is a very important ceremony. It marks a new stage for the boy and the start of his adult life. He must wear the cotton thread throughout his life, looped over his left shoulder and under his right arm.

Some weddings are blessed in the marriage hall at the *mandir*. Others are held at home. Many Hindus marry someone recommended for them by their family. If the boy and girl agree, and their horoscopes are well matched, the marriage can go ahead. The priest chooses a day and the invitations are sent out.

A Hindu marriage is not binding until seven steps have been taken around the sacred fire.

A Hindu wedding lasts several days, with many ceremonies and rituals. On the wedding day itself, the bride puts on a special red silk sari and elaborate jewellery and make-up. She and the groom sit in front of the sacred fire while the priest recites prayers and guides them through the ceremony. There are 15 rituals to perform, including taking seven steps around the fire. At each step, the couple take a vow. After the wedding, the bride usually goes to live with her husband and his family.

here are many ***mandirs*** *in India dedicated to* ▶
ord Swaminarayan, particularly in Gujarat,
here the Swaminarayan Movement was founded.

aranasi is one of the most sacred places of pilgrimage.
ccording to legend, the great god Shiva chose the city
s his home on Earth. Many of the city's ***mandirs*** *are*
edicated to Shiva.

When Hindus die, their bodies are cremated, on a funeral pyre or in a crematorium. If possible, their ashes are taken to India and scattered in the sacred River Ganges. Twelve days of mourning follow, with prayers for the dead person's soul and its future rebirth.

The River Ganges is the Hindus' holiest river. They believe that its water has the power to wash away their sins. Every year, millions of pilgrims flock to the sacred city of Varanasi, which stands on the banks of the river in northern India, to bathe and scatter the ashes of dead relations in the water.

Holy books

Hindus read and study many different sacred texts as part of their worship and as guides for living their lives. The oldest texts are called the *Vedas*. These are collections of hymns, prayers and magic spells, which are more than 3,500 years old. The holiest Veda is the *Rig Veda*, the "Song of Knowledge". It contains 1,028 hymns in praise of the gods.

At first, the sacred texts were learned by heart and passed on by word of mouth. Later, they were written down in Sanskrit, the sacred language of India. This ancient manuscript is written in Sanskrit.

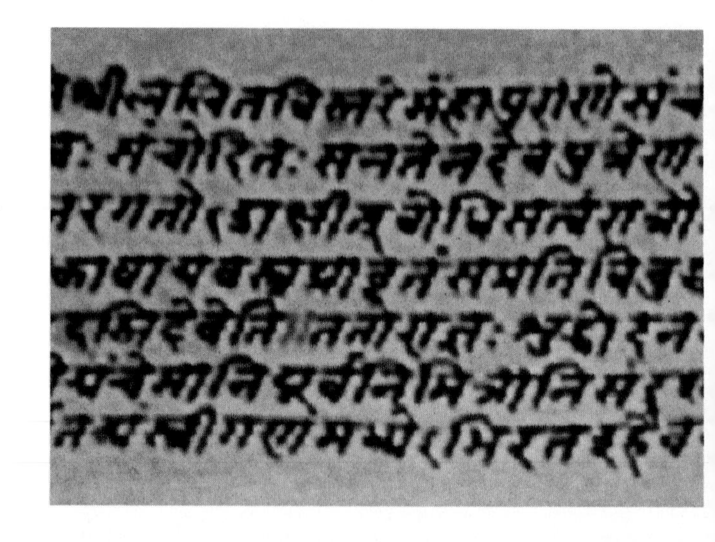

The second group of scriptures are called the *Upanishads*. Composed in about 800BCE, they take the form of sacred lessons taught by gurus to their pupils and talk about the relationship between people's souls and God.

Dylan read from one of the sacred texts which had been placed in a special, wooden stand.

Here the Guru reads from the sacred texts. The most sacred is the ***Vachanamrut****. This is a collection of 262 discourses, or talks, given by Lord Swaminarayan. They were written down as he spoke.*

The other most important texts are two long poems, the *Mahabharata* and the *Ramayana*. The *Mahabharata* tells of a war between two rival families, the Kauravas and Pandavas. The most popular part of the story, called the *Bhagavad Gita*, or the "Song of the Lord", is set on the battlefield. In it, the deity Krishna reminds Arjuna, one of the Pandavas, that he must do his duty without thinking of himself. This is one of the key aims of Hinduism.

A scene from the ***Ramayana****. Rama is shown killing Ravana, watched by Hanuman.*

Time-line

This time-line shows some of the most important dates in the history of Hinduism and the key events leading up to the building of the Shri Swaminarayan *Mandir* in London. The dates are written as BCE (Before the Common Era) and CE (Common Era), a dating system which is shared by members of different religions.

c. 2,500 BCE
The Indus Valley Civilisation is at its height. Its two centres are the great cities of Harappa and Mohenjo Daro.

c. 1,500 BCE
The ideas of the Aryan people living around the River Sindhu mix with those of the Indus Valley to form the basis of Hinduism.

c. 1,500 BCE-1,000 BCE
The *Vedas*, the oldest Hindu sacred texts, are used by Aryan priests in their rites and ceremonies.

c. 800-400 BCE
The *Upanishads* are composed. But they are not written down for hundreds of years.

1600s CE
The British and other Europeans begin to bring Christianity to India.

1781 CE
Lord Swaminarayan is born in India on 3 April. At the age of 11, he leaves his home on a holy journey around India. He settles in Gujarat and founds the Swaminarayan Movement.

1830 CE
Lord Swaminarayan passes away on 1 June.

1869 CE
Birth of Mahatma Gandhi, one of India's greatest spiritual and political leaders. He is assassinated in 1948.

1921 CE
Birth of Pramukh Swami Maharaj, the present Guru of the Swaminarayan Movement.

1947 CE
India wins independence from its British rulers. It is divided up into Hindu India and Muslim Pakistan.

1950s-1960s CE
Many Hindus leave India to work and settle in Britain and North America.

1990 CE
The Swaminarayan Movement acquires a plot of land in London for building a new *mandir*. It is to be built in traditional Hindu style.

c. 500 BCE

Two other religions – Buddhism and Jainism – are founded in India. Many ordinary people turn to them from Hinduism.

300 BCE-300 CE

Large parts of the *Mahabharata* and *Ramayana* are composed. These two long poems are still the most popular Hindu sacred texts.

c. 320-550 CE

The Gupta kings rule much of India. This period becomes known as the "Golden Age" of Hinduism. Hindu culture and religion flourishes.

1001 CE

Muslims begin to invade India from the north-west and to spread their own Islamic religion through the country.

THE MANY HEADS OF RAVANA, THE DEMON KING, FROM THE RAMAYANA

1469 CE

Guru Nanak, the founder of the Sikh religion, is born in India.

1500s CE

Worship of Lord Rama and Lord Krishna becomes very popular.

1526 CE

The beginning of the Mughal Empire in India. The Mughal emperors are Muslims. One of the greatest emperors, Akbar, forms his own religion by mixing Muslim, Hindu and Christian ideas.

1570s CE

The great poet, Tulsi Das, writes a very famous version of the *Ramayana*, called the *Ram Charit Manas*.

RAMA

KRISHNA

1993 CE

The first carved stones arrive from India. Building of the Cultural Complex (attached to the *mandir*) begins.

1992 CE

In August, on Krishna's birthday, the site for the new *mandir* is cleared. Building begins in November. Bulgarian and Italian marble and limestone are shipped to India to be carved.

1991 CE

Pramukh Swami Maharaj visits London and lays the foundation stone for the new *mandir*.

1995 CE

On 18 August, the images for the *mandir* are carried through London as part of a huge and colourful procession. On 20 August, Pramukh Swami Maharaj performs a ceremony to install the sacred images in the *mandir*. The Shri Swaminarayan *Mandir* is officially open!

THE MANDIR AT NEASDEN

How to find out more

Visiting the mandir

Everyone is welcome to visit the Sri Swaminarayan Mandir at 105/119 Brentfield Road, Neasden, London NW10 8JP
Tel: 020 8965 2651 Fax: 020 8965 6313
Website: www.swaminarayan.org

You should phone the *mandir* to book a guided tour. Ask about the best time to see the sacred images in the inner sanctum, as they are not on view all the time.

When you visit, treat the *mandir* with care and respect. Don't wear shorts or short skirts and don't take food or drink into the *mandir*. Photography is not allowed inside but you can take photos of the outside. When you go in, you must take off your shoes and leave your coat and bag in the cloakroom.

To find out the location of your nearest *mandir*, look in the places of worship section of your telephone directory, or contact your local SACRE (Standing Advisory Council for Religious Education). You could also visit the Global Network section of www.swaminarayan.org

Making a Hindu collection

Putting together a collection of Hindu objects and artefacts in your classroom is a good way of learning more about Hinduism. There are many Indian shops in Britain (particularly in the big cities, such as London, Bradford and Leicester) which stock these objects. The *mandir* also has many sacred objects for sale. The following objects will give you a good starter collection. But you can add or change objects as you go along.

For a basic collection, you may need:

Plastic images of the gods or goddesses. You can also buy postcards and paintings.
Metal *Om* symbol
Incense sticks (joss sticks) for *puja*
Prayer-beads (*mala*)
Diwali card
Metal *puja* set (which includes a tray, bell, lamp, incense-burner, tumbler and spoon)
Red powder for *chandlo* (called *kum kum* powder)

Useful words

arti A ceremony in which a tray of lamps is offered to the sacred images as a sign of welcome. Often performed at the beginning or end of *puja*.
amrita A magic potion, believed to give the gift of everlasting life to those who drink it.
archaeologist Someone who studies the past by looking at ancient objects and ruined buildings.
Aryan The Aryans were people who lived in north-west India in about 1500 BCE.
bhajans Hymns or songs sung in praise of God.
chandlo A red mark of blessing made on worshippers' foreheads during *puja*.
consort Another name for a husband or wife.
cremated Hindus are cremated, or burnt to ashes, when they die.
darshana The viewing or seeing of the images in the *mandir*.
deity Another name for a god, goddess or sacred figure.
ghee A type of butter used in Indian cooking.
guru A great spiritual teacher, leader and holy man.
horoscope A chart showing the position of the stars and planets at the time of a person's birth. Used by astrologers and priests to tell a person's future.
incarnation God appearing in human form on Earth.
inner sanctum The inner-most and holiest shrine of the *mandir* where the sacred images stand.
karma A person's actions and the results of those actions, good or bad. Your karma determines how you will be reborn.
mandir A place where Hindus go to worship. Often called a temple.
Moksha The aim of a Hindu's life. The freedom of the soul from the continuous cycle of birth, death and rebirth.
Murti The sacred image of a deity or holy man which stands in the inner sanctum of the *mandir*. The image represents an aspect or incarnation of God.
Om A sacred sound, often chanted at the beginning and end of prayers, and during meditation. It symbolises the sound of creation.
Para Brahman The supreme spirit, or God. Everything comes from Para Brahman and eventually returns to Para Brahman.
pilgrimage A special journey to a sacred place to worship, ask for a favour or give thanks.
prasad The gifts of food, flowers and incense offered to the sacred images during *puja*.
Puja The main Hindu form of worship, performed in the *mandir* or at home. Prayers and prasad are offered to the sacred images.
Pujaris Priests who carry out the *puja* ceremony. Only they are allowed to approach the sacred images.
rituals Religious ceremonies.
sacred Another word for holy.
Sadhus Hindu holy men who have given up their families and possessions to dedicate themselves to God.
Sanatana dharma The eternal teaching or eternal law. This is how Hindus think of their religion.
scriptures Holy books or texts.
shrine A place of worship, either in a *mandir* or at home.
Swami A title given to a great religious teacher or holy man.
swastika The ancient Hindu sign of peace and good luck. It was twisted round by the German Nazis during World War II to become their symbol of evil.
Vegetarians People who do not eat meat.

Index

Reprinted 2002, 2006
First paperback edition 2000

First published 1998
A & C Black Publishers Ltd
38 Soho Square, London W1D 3HB
www.acblack.com

ISBN-10: 0-7136-5495-3
ISBN-13: 978-0-7136-5495-0

A CIP catalogue record for this book is available from the British Library.

Acknowledgements
The author and publisher would like to thank Ciara, Dylan and James and all concerned at the Shri Swaminarayan Mandir for their generous help in the preparation of this book.

All Photographs reproduced by kind permission of the Swaminarayan Hindu Mission apart from: pp 2a, 3b, 5b, 6 (both), 7b, 12, 13a, 16a, 17b, 18a, 21b, 26b, 30 (both) Jak Kilby; p 4 CM Dixon; pp 5a, 13b, 21a, 25a, 27b Ann & Bury Peerless; pp 11b, 17a, 19 TRIP Photo Library: p 24 David Rose; p 26a Ancient Art and Architecture Collection.

All artwork by Vanessa Card

A & C Black uses paper produced with elemental chlorine-free pulp, harvested from managed sustainable forests.

Printed in China by WKT Company Ltd.